POUND THE STONE
TRAINING MANUAL

Joshua Medcalf

ISBN: 1546770224
ISBN 13: 9781546770220

DESIGN

THIS TRAINING MANUAL was designed first and foremost to be a personal introspective journey to take a deeper dive into the wisdom presented in *Pound The Stone*. It was not designed to be a group discussion guide. However, we do believe it can be used as such with a skilled discussion leader.

You do need to have a copy of the book, *Pound The Stone*, in order to fully maximize this training manual as it breaks each chapter down into questions to reflect upon after reading.

ENOUGH IS ENOUGH

Have you ever made a decision out of anger that ended up creating a lot more pain and setbacks in your life? Describe the decision. What was the outcome?

_____

_____

_____

_____

What did that decision cost you financially/spiritually/relationally/emotionally?

_____

_____

_____

_____

If you find yourself in a similar situation, what are two or three things you could do to better manage your emotions so you don't end up making a tough situation worse?

_____

_____

_____

_____

LAST CHANCE

Have you ever gotten a second chance you didn't deserve? What happened?

_____

_____

_____

_____

Have you ever had someone step up and vouch for you when you were in a tough spot?

_____

_____

How did it make you feel when that person vouched for you?

_____

_____

_____

What did you learn from the experience?

_____

_____

_____

_____

KAIYA

Have you ever met someone who was very different from anyone you had ever met in a very good way? Describe their character traits.

_____

_____

_____

_____

What was it about them that made them unique?

_____

_____

_____

_____

POUND THE STONE

"When nothing seems to help, I go and look at a stonecutter hammering away at his rock perhaps a hundred times without as much as a crack showing in it. Yet at the hundred and first blow it will split in two, and I know it was not that blow that did it, but all that had gone before." –Jacob Riis

What does the Stonecutter's Credo mean to you?

_____

_____

_____

_____

What do you think T.D. means when he says, "Everyone wants to be great, until it's time to do what greatness requires?"

_____

_____

_____

_____

T.D. says, "*Talent is overrated.* But the ability to pound the stone, day in and day out, year after year, until finally the stone splits? *That is the rarest, most valuable asset on the planet.*" Do you think is true? Where have you seen this in your world?

_____

_____

_____

_____

Who do you hope to become through the process you are currently going through? Specifically, what characteristics do you hope to develop?

_____

_____

_____

_____

Commitment Card: Week 1

Start Date: _____   End Date: _____

What are you willing to commit to doing this week to help you develop the skills and characteristics you hope to gain through the process? Make sure you are specific as possible, and that each commitment is 100% controllable.

Make sure you have at least one characteristic such as grit, patience, courage, love, empathy, growth mindset, self-awareness, or persistence. Make sure you have one skill as well.

For example, if you hope to develop courage, you might put, "I commit to doing one thing that scares me every day this week." If you hope to develop empathy, you might put, "I commit to taking a few minutes to think about all the tough stuff most likely going on in each person's life who frustrates me this week."

If you hope to develop your ball handling skills, you might put, "15 min before practice of doing ball handing drills at game speed." If you hope to develop your sales business, you might put, "Write and mail 25 thank you cards." Another example would be, "Make at least 25 prospective client calls per day."

I want to develop this characteristic:

_____

In order to help ensure that I develop that I am going to commit to:

_____

_____

_____

I want to develop this characteristic:

_____

In order to help ensure that I develop that I am going to commit to:

_____

_____

_____

I want to develop this skill:

_____

In order to help ensure that I develop that I am going to commit to:

_____

_____

_____

I want to develop this skill:

_____

In order to help ensure that I develop that I am going to commit to:

_____

_____

_____

THE SMALLEST HOUSE ON THE BLOCK

Have you ever experienced a time when you were really motivated at the beginning of something, but after a little bit of time, you were frustrated and ready to give up?

_____

_____

_____

What are specific things you can focus on to help maintain motivation to persist in spite of your feelings?

_____

_____

_____

Have you ever quit something because of your temporary feelings and then later regretted it?

_____

_____

_____

What motivates you to persevere when you are ready to give up?

_____

_____

_____

DO IT ANYWAY

In this chapter, Russ says, "One thing I've learned on my journey is that you are never truly ready. The only way you get prepared and ready is by actually experiencing the thing you are afraid of doing, but that you know in your gut you are supposed to do. The timing will never be right. There is no such thing as perfect timing." Share what this means to you.

_____

_____

_____

What are some of your 'What if's' that would be more beneficial if you turned them into 'Even if's'? Some examples might be: I don't get into the colleges I want. I don't get the job. I don't get a sports scholarship. I get fired. I get rejected.

Even if _____

I will _____.

Even if _____

I will _____.

Even if _____

I will _____.

Even if _____

I will _____.

Russ tells Jason to view his life as a story. "Start to see your life as a story Jason, and remember that every great story has plot twists, trials and hardships. We love stories where the unlikely hero overcomes adversity and chooses to act in spite of facing seemingly impossible odds." What are your favorite stories? What would change in your life if you started to see your life this way? What are some of the plot twists in your life?

_____
_____
_____
_____
_____
_____

Conor McGregor says, "I never lose: either I win, or I learn." Hopefully, you will learn when you win as well, but what would your life look like if believed you could never lose? Reflect on a specific time when you gained more from a "loss" than from a "win". What were some of the "wins" that came from that "loss".

_____
_____
_____
_____
_____
_____

How would adopting the growth mindset of believing everything that has happened in the past is in your best interest and an opportunity to learn and grow free you up during pressure situations?

_____

_____

_____

_____

_____

_____

Russ tells Jason, "There will always be obstacles, setbacks, and legitimate excuses not to do what you know in your gut you should do. <u>Do it any-way</u>." What are some things that you need to "do it anyway" in spite of your legitimate excuses?

_____

_____

_____

DEFINING SUCCESS

What was your take away from the story about Dave?

_____

_____

_____

What does this quote mean to you? *"Our greatest fear in life should not be of failure, but of succeeding at things in life that don't really matter."* –Francis Chan

_____

_____

_____

Are there any things in your life that *"don't really matter"* that you are putting time and energy into?

_____

_____

_____

What do you want to be remembered for when you are gone?

_____

_____

_____

Are there 2-3 specific changes you need to make in your life to ensure that you will be remembered for what you wrote above when you are gone?

_____

_____

_____

CUT THE ROPES

What was your takeaway from the story about the elephants and the ropes?

_____

_____

_____

What are the ropes in your life that have been holding you back?

_____

_____

_____

"We learn our belief systems as very little children and then move through life creating experiences to match our beliefs." –Louise Hay

What beliefs are you clinging to that are keeping you stuck?

_____

_____

_____

What are some false beliefs that you have seen be disproved in your life? This could be by you, or by others. Something you or others believed was true, but then you saw evidence to the contrary?

_____

_____

_____

PAPER CEILINGS

On a scale of 1-10 how much do you enjoy training and practice? What do you think is behind this?

_____

_____

_____

What were your takeaways from the story about the five year old boy named Garrett?

_____

_____

_____

Russ tells Jason, "When someone tells you something is 'impossible,' what that really means is that it would take more sacrifice, grit, discipline, failure, and persistence then they are willing to give." Have you ever seen this to be true?

_____

_____

_____

What are some of the paper ceilings you have broken through in your life?

_____

_____

_____

_____

_____

_____

What is an example of someone you know breaking through a paper ceiling?

_____

_____

_____

What are some of the paper ceilings that are holding you back in life right now?

_____

_____

_____

Russ tells Jason, "Our world has perpetually been driven forward by those people, the ones who have believed the impossible was possible with grit, trust, and patience, and who were willing to take responsibility for what they have control over." Who are some examples of people who have done this? Try to think of at least one person you know personally, and at least one person you have learned about (books, movies, etc.)

_____

_____

_____

INCHES AND NAILS

Have you ever been late and it ended up costing you something important to you? What did you learn through this experience?

_____

_____

_____

T.D. tells Jason, "Life and basketball are determined by inches. Lots of small, seemingly insignificant things, that added up and compounded over time will determine the trajectory of your life. Most people focus on all the big stuff, failing to realize it is the little stuff that makes all the difference." What are some of the small things you have seen make a big difference?

_____

_____

_____

_____

_____

_____

What did you learn from the story of Napoleon and the Battle of Waterloo?

_____

_____

_____

What are some of the small things you need to refocus on?

_____

_____

_____

Commitment Card: Week 2

Start Date: _____ End Date: _____

What did you learn from the week 1 commitment card?

_____

_____

_____

What changes do you need to make to ensure this weeks commitments go better?

_____

_____

_____

I want to develop this characteristic:

_____

In order to help ensure that I develop that I am going to commit to:

_____

_____

_____

I want to develop this characteristic:

_____

In order to help ensure that I develop that I am going to commit to:

_____

_____

_____

I want to develop this skill:

_____

In order to help ensure that I develop that I am going to commit to:

_____

_____

_____

I want to develop this skill:

_____

In order to help ensure that I develop that I am going to commit to:

_____

_____

_____

FOCUS ON YOUR STRENGTHS

Russ let out a little laugh, "Earlier in my life I would have. But over time, I've become a bigger believer in the opposite: going all in on your strengths. A researcher named Marcus Buckingham conducted interviews with thousands of the best business managers in the world, and what his research found is that you grow the most in the areas of your strength. So while I know you might have heard otherwise all your life, I think that if you focus on your strengths, you simply become average at a lot of things, but the master of none. Mastery is hard and it takes a lot of time, effort, and energy. So if you have limited components of each of those, you should probably spend what you do have on what you're best at."

What are at least three specific strengths that you have? How do you know?

_____

_____

_____

What percent of your time is spent on improving your strengths? Weaknesses?

_____

_____

_____

MAINTANING THE MASK

"Oh, I do. But I call it something else, Jason." Russ's eyes grew clear and intense. "I don't call it 'not losing face.' I call it 'maintaining the mask,' and it's the same reason you won't be honest with me about how worried you really are about your Mom right now." Jason shifted uncomfortably, not knowing what to say. Russ went on, "Our culture has taught you that as a young man, you can never authentically show any feeling other than anger. Unfortunately, anger is a secondary emotion. It always comes from something else. But showing anything else is seen as weakness. So your two choices are to be seen as weak, or to get angry. Does that sound about right?" Russ explains the power in vulnerability and the cultural practice to mask emotion. While people maintain the mask to look strong, Russ shares with Jason that removing the mask and being real truly indicates a strong person.

Do you believe people "maintain the mask" in your circle? How do they do this?

_____

_____

_____

_____

_____

Like discussing Jason's dad, what is something you avoid confronting because it makes you feel vulnerable?

_____

_____

_____

PRISON

"Well, it's hard to believe you could just walk away from prison and pursue your dreams and destiny. Most people would rather believe someone else is keeping them chained up, than accept the truth: the only one responsible for keeping us where we are, is us. Everyone has challenges. Some see them as an excuse, but the rare few choose to see them for what they really are; the forging ground for greatness. When you've been stuck in prison for most of your life, it is hard to believe that the world is full of endless opportunities. But our world is no longer a prison: it's a meritocracy. The internet, social media, and amazing advancements in technology have made it possible for anyone who is willing to pound the stone and willing to consistently hit publish to reach the entire world."

Who is someone that you know who continues to work in a job that they hate? What is this person like to be around? Why do you believe they stay?

_____

_____

_____

Who is someone that you know who has a job that they love? What is this person like to be around?

_____

_____

_____

STOP COUNTING

Russ looked at Jason with empathy as he recognized that same ambition in himself. Ambition that had almost derailed him at many points along his own journey. "Jason, one of the wisest things I've learned is that with your eyes on the goal, you have no eyes for the journey. I understand that you think you know where you want to get to, but it's the process that gets us there. It's all the little things. When you focus on every thing other than your journey, you are more likely to get lost and end up far from your desired destination."

What are at least five habits that you commit to that make up your "process?"

_____

_____

_____

What are at least three goals that you intentionally avoid focusing on?

_____

_____

_____

What is an example of a time when you lost sight of the process and focused on goals? How did this work out for you?

_____

_____

_____

1%

"Back in 2010, a guy named Dave Brailsford was tasked with a serious challenge. He had just taken over England's cycling team, a team that had never won a Tour de France. Dave had a unique strategy though. Rather than focusing on big goals like winning a Tour de France, he was going to focus on improving the little things – everything from the way the team washed their hands, all the way to the type of pillow they slept on– by just 1%. He believed that if they could just improve everything by 1%, then through the power of small aggregated gains they should be able to win the Tour De France in five years."

Jason leaned forward, hooked. "So, did he do it?"

"No. Turns out, Dave was wrong: they won it in just three years."

What are at least five areas that you could improve by 1%? List them below and how you could improve them.

_____

_____

_____

_____

_____

_____

YOU, INC.

Jan looked at him with empathy, "Well, the most important little thing is one that takes place internally, and it's your heart posture. Are you there to give or to get? Are you there to close a sale, or to give someone an opportunity to learn something that could change their life?"

"The truth is, Jason, the world will only take you as seriously as you take yourself. Until you take yourself seriously, how can you expect anyone else to take you seriously? Be honest with me, would you buy a book from you right now? Do you trust you? Are you dressed like someone you can trust? Do you speak like someone you would trust?"

Jason fell silent as her questions rolled around in his mind. "Here, maybe this is a better way to sum it up. Would you hire yourself for a $250,000 a year job right now?"

Jan asks Jason the tough questions above. How would you have answered? Would you hire yourself for a $250,000 a year job? What are at least three reasons you would use as evidence to support your argument.

_____

_____

_____

_____

_____

_____

Commitment Card: Week 3

Start Date: _____ End Date: _____

What did you learn from the week 2 commitment card?

_____

_____

_____

What changes do you need to make to ensure this weeks' commitments go better?

_____

_____

_____

I want to develop this characteristic:

_____

In order to help ensure that I develop that I am going to commit to:

_____

_____

_____

I want to develop this characteristic:

_____

In order to help ensure that I develop that I am going to commit to:

_____

_____

_____

I want to develop this skill:

_____

In order to help ensure that I develop that I am going to commit to:

_____

_____

_____

I want to develop this skill:

_____

In order to help ensure that I develop that I am going to commit to:

_____

_____

_____

What was your best failure this week?

_____

_____

_____

If you could do this week over, what would you do differently?

_____

_____

_____

A WEALTH OF WISDOM

If you went to court, would there be enough evidence to convict you of investing in yourself and taking yourself seriously? What evidence would you present?

_____

_____

_____

_____

_____

_____

Think about and list out at least three things in your life that fall into the category of "easy to do, easier not to do"?

_____

_____

_____

_____

_____

_____

GRIT

Who are 5 people you look up to who will give you honest feedback?

_____

_____

_____

_____

_____

_____

What are your external choices (clothing, haricut, piercings, etc) communicating to the world around you? Are they repelling or attracting the type of opportunities you want?

_____

_____

_____

How would you define grit?

_____

_____

_____

Why do you think grit is a better predictor of future success then things like talent, intelligence, family status, or aptitude tests?

_____

_____

_____

What was the best failure you had this week?

_____
_____
_____

If you could do today over again, what would you do differently?

_____
_____
_____

Gary Vee says, "One is greater than zero." What does that mean to you? How can you apply that philosophy in your life? What are the biggest obstacles to applying that in your life?

_____
_____
_____
_____
_____

Jan tells Jason, "there is no such thing as microwaveable mastery." Where do you need to spend more time to develop mastery instead of seeking out the microwaveable mastery?

_____
_____
_____
_____

SIDES TO A BOX

Have you ever felt like someone else has a "perfect" life, only to find out that it isn't so great when you start to pull back the layers?

_____

_____

What happens when you fall for the comparison trap?

_____

_____

Russ tells the guys, "In life we often forget that what we see isn't always all there is, and that there are always more sides to everything and everyone. Every person and every event in our lives is multi-dimensional. Just because we aren't aware of them, doesn't mean those sides don't exist." How have you seen this play out, and what are the implications for your life?

_____

_____

_____

_____

Russ tells the guys, "What you see in your environment is not reality, it is simply your perception of reality. If you are open to changing your perspective, you might find an amazing reality has been awaiting you, _in your exact same environment._" What are your thoughts about this?

_____

_____

_____

_____

In what areas of your life could you potentially benefit from being more open minded?

_____

_____

PERSISTENCE

Do you believe in luck? Why?

_____

_____

_____

_____

Kaiya tells Jason, *"You can keep that luck in your pocket. Haven't you seen Man on Fire? There's only two kinds of people, trained and untrained, and I'm trained. Luck is for people that haven't trained to be clutch. I don't need luck"* What would change in your life if you stopped believing in luck, and focused on taken responsibility for your training and everything you have 100% control over, and surrendered the rest?

_____

_____

_____

_____

_____

_____

_____

_____

_____

"WHAT DO YOU KNOW?"

What does "surrender the outcome" mean to you?

_____

_____

_____

Have you ever focused on the little things and surrender the outcome, but things still didn't seem to be going the way you would like?

_____

_____

_____

Warren Buffet said, "the chains of habit are too light to feel until they are too heavy to be broken". What does this mean to you? Have you ever seen this in your life or someone you love?

_____

_____

_____

Russ tells Jason, "these are the moments where true grit is developed. These moments when it feels like everything inside of you is screaming to quit. In these moments of inescapable frustration, that is where true grit is built on the path to mastery. This moment is an amazing opportunity to develop the grit you're going to need in crucial moments of your life down the road. I know you think you want to quit, but this choice will impact the rest of your life." Do you agree with this? What makes you feel that way?

_____

_____

_____

Commitment Card: Week 4

Start Date: _____ End Date: _____

What did you learn from last weeks' commitment card?

_____

_____

_____

What changes do you need to make to ensure this weeks' commitments go better?

_____

_____

_____

I want to develop this characteristic:

_____

In order to help ensure that I develop that I am going to commit to:

_____

_____

_____

I want to develop this characteristic:

_____

In order to help ensure that I develop that I am going to commit to:

_____

_____

_____

I want to develop this skill:

_____

In order to help ensure that I develop that I am going to commit to:

_____

_____

_____

I want to develop this skill:

_____

In order to help ensure that I develop that I am going to commit to:

_____

_____

_____

What was your best failure this week?

_____

_____

_____

If you could do this week over, what would you do differently?

_____

_____

_____

AUSTIN

Have you ever misjudged someone because of what you thought they did for a living? Can you give an example?

_____

_____

_____

What was your takeaway from learning that Russ wasn't just a street sweeper?

_____

_____

_____

Martin Luther King Jr. said, "If a man is called to be a street sweeper, he should sweep streets even as Michaelangelo painted, or Beethoven composed music or Shakespeare wrote poetry. He should sweep streets so well that all the hosts of heaven and earth will pause to say, 'Here lived a great street sweeper who did his job well." Reflect on this quote and Russ's life. What are the implications for your life?

_____

_____

_____

_____

_____

_____

_____

BUILD WISELY

What did you learn from the story of Kota building his own house?

_____

_____

_____

Create a New Scorecard for your life. Choose 3 to 4 characteristics you want to grade yourself on twice per day, once at lunch and again before bed.

Characteristic: _____

Grade: _____

Characteristic: _____

Grade: _____

Characteristic: _____

Grade: _____

Characteristic: _____

Grade: _____

*Bonus (Get your new scorecard printed and laminated on a 3-5 note-card that you carry with you throughout your day.)

FAILURE

When is a time that you experienced "failure" that ended up helping you grow your character more than "success" would have?

_____

_____

_____

Where in your life can you create an environment where you are able to get used to hearing the word "no" a lot, so it stops scaring you so much?

_____

_____

_____

What could happen in your life if you stopped worrying about "failure" or hearing "no"? What are at least three things you would do if you were not afraid of failing or someone saying no.

_____

_____

_____

Caroline tells Jason that, "Failure is an event, not an identity." She also says that "if you want to hit a lot of home runs, you have to be willing to strike out a lot." What are some practical ways you can start to put yourself out there and swing for the fences, while simultaneously knowing you are going to strike out more?

_____

_____

_____

DOOR TO DOOR

Do you think that developing grit and character is more important than achieving your short term goals? What have you experienced that has caused you to feel this way?

_____

_____

_____

Have you ever given up during the middle of something, only to come so much closer than you ever would have thought at the end?

_____

_____

_____

What did you learn through that experience?

_____

_____

_____

EARLY HOURS

Coach Michael said to Jason, "some opportunities have an expiration date." Have you ever experienced this in your life?

_____

_____

_____

Have you ever experienced people expecting you to fail and not follow through on your commitment? How did that make you feel?

_____

_____

_____

Commitment Card: Week 5

Start Date: _____ End Date: _____

I want to develop this characteristic:

_____

In order to help ensure that I develop that I am going to commit to:

_____

_____

_____

I want to develop this characteristic:

_____

In order to help ensure that I develop that I am going to commit to:

_____

_____

_____

I want to develop this skill:

_____

In order to help ensure that I develop that I am going to commit to:

_____

_____

_____

I want to develop this skill:

_____

In order to help ensure that I develop that I am going to commit to:

_____

_____

_____

What was your best failure this week?

_____

_____

_____

If you could do this week over, what would you do differently?

_____

_____

_____

—————————— ⌒ ——————————

Have you ever found yourself in a position like Jason, not knowing if all the hard work you were putting in was going to work?

_____

_____

_____

Kaiya tells Jason, "hard work is the price of admission for the opportunity to become great at anything, not just basketball. Business, creativity, relationships. Greatness takes resilience. Mastery takes grit." What are your thoughts about this?

_____

_____

_____

What is an example of a time you let a moment of temporary pain push you into making a poor decision?

_____

_____

_____

What did that end up costing you?

_____

_____

_____

If you find yourself in a similar situation, what do you think you could do differently?

_____

_____

_____

Have you ever had a friend show up and work with you in the trenches when you needed it most? Take five minutes and write them or call them to tell them how much that meant to you, and how much you appreciate their friendship.

LOSING SEASON

Have you ever had someone vouch for you in a tough spot? How did that make you feel?

_____

_____

_____

What is an area of your life that you know you need to 'pound the stone' but you are afraid of putting in the work with no guaranteed outcome?

_____

_____

_____

What could it cost you if you keep going down the same path you are currently on?

_____

_____

_____

"TRAVIS..."

Jason goes through the greatest challenge of his life by losing one of his best friends, Travis. Do you have an example of a time when somebody that you love passed away unexpectantly?

_____

_____

_____

Instead of taking his own life, what options could Travis have chosen to overcome the challenge he was facing?

_____

_____

_____

Who is someone you know that is held to "a higher standard" like Travis was? What are the benefits of these higher expectations? What can be the dangers?

_____

_____

_____

AN ANCHOR FOR YOUR SOUL

During the storms in your life, what serves as your anchor? How do you maintain the courage to make it through?

_____

_____

_____

What do you do to cope with challenging situations in a positive and beneficial way?

_____

_____

_____

READ CHAPTER 31

MOVING ON

When is a time when you experienced pain in overcoming a challenge like Jason?

_____

_____

_____

Who is someone like Russ that has comforted you in challenging times by being present? How did this person do it?

_____

_____

_____

What do the words, "I am with you" mean to you? Why do you think that they are so powerful to Jason in that moment?

_____

_____

_____

Commitment Card: Week 6

Start Date: _____ End Date: _____

I want to develop this characteristic:

_____

In order to help ensure that I develop that I am going to commit to:

_____

_____

_____

I want to develop this characteristic:

_____

In order to help ensure that I develop that I am going to commit to:

_____

_____

_____

I want to develop this skill:

_____

In order to help ensure that I develop that I am going to commit to:

_____

_____

_____

I want to develop this skill:

_____

In order to help ensure that I develop that I am going to commit to:

_____

_____

_____

What was your best failure this week?

_____

_____

_____

If you could do this week over, what would you do differently?

_____

_____

_____

BRING YOUR BASKETBALL

Who is a friend that has helped you through a difficult time like Kaiya helps Jason through? Specifically, how did this friend help you?

_____

_____

_____

What did that mean to you when this person stepped up in your life like that?

_____

_____

_____

When is an example of a time when you helped a friend through a difficult time? What did you do to help this friend?

_____

_____

_____

LAYERS AND LIGHT

Have you ever met someone like Ryan whose perspective and the way they loved radically impacted your life?

_____

_____

_____

How can you do a better job of valuing and treasuring every single moment you have with people?

_____

_____

_____

Kaiya tells Jason, "In order to experience the joy of a child, we have to be willing to open ourselves up again and let our light shine bright. *When we shine the way we are intended to, not with arrogance, but with authentic joy, peace, wholeness, and contentment, we allow others to slowly peel back their layers and shine as well.*" What are some of the things you block others from seeing in you because of past hurts and fear?

_____

_____

_____

_____

_____

_____

_____

THE PATH TO MASTERY

Why do you think you would develop more character in a door to door sales program then in a classroom setting?

_____

_____

_____

What were your thoughts after seeing the Rory put up the diagram of how the path to mastery actually works? Describe a time when you've seen someone's experience match Rory's diagram of the path to mastery.

_____

_____

_____

Rory said that one of the keys to your success is to "Find your uniqueness and exploit it in the service of others." What does this mean to you? What could that be for you? Try and find a few people who you admire and who hold you in high regard and tell them the quote and ask them what that could be for you.

_____

_____

_____

_____

_____

_____

DAVID BEFORE GOLIATH

T.D. tells Jason, if you can't master the basics, you'll never be able to master anything bigger. What are some of the basics you need to spend more time mastering?

_____

_____

_____

Have you ever had an experience where if you had known it was coming you would have prepared differently? How did this impact how you prepare today?

_____

_____

_____

If you knew you were going to get the opportunity of your dreams in six months to a year, how would you use your 86,400 seconds today?

_____

_____

_____

What was your takeaways from the David and Goliath story T.D. told Jason. Had you ever thought about David's faithfulness tending sheep as preparation for that moment?

_____

_____

_____

T.D. tells Jason, "if you truly fall in love with the process, you will **eventually** love what the process produces." What does this mean to you? Describe a time when you have been tempted to quit, or did quit because the process wasn't producing what you wanted quick enough?

_____

_____

_____

BLAME VS. RESPONSIBILITY

Jan tells Jason, "When you pull back the layers on the people who have lived extraordinary lives you rarely find a silver spoon or childhood prodigy. Occasionally, you do, but more often than not you find people who decided to do the very best they could, with what they had, right where they were at." What does this mean to you?

_____

_____

_____

"Our culture is obsessed with eliminating struggle. There are parents whose goal is that their kids want for nothing. But what if they're handicapping them instead? Our fear of failure for the next generation is creating people primed for mediocrity at best and crippled at worst, in comparison to their potential. *Experiencing repeated failure and lack of resources forces you to develop deep levels of grit, intellectual creativity, and resourcefulness others have never tapped into.*" Do you agree or disagree with this passage? Explain why.

_____

_____

_____

_____

_____

_____

What is the difference between blame and responsibility?

_____

_____

_____

Jan tells Jason, *"The most valuable things in life you can't be given, and they can't be bought. No amount of money, family status, or talent can buy character and grit... they can only be earned."* What are your thoughts about this?

_____

_____

_____

Commitment Card: Week 7

Start Date: _____ End Date: _____

I want to develop this characteristic:

_____

In order to help ensure that I develop that I am going to commit to:

_____

_____

_____

I want to develop this characteristic:

_____

In order to help ensure that I develop that I am going to commit to:

_____

_____

_____

I want to develop this skill:

_____

In order to help ensure that I develop that I am going to commit to:

_____

_____

_____

I want to develop this skill:

_____

In order to help ensure that I develop that I am going to commit to:

_____
_____
_____

What was your best failure this week?

_____
_____
_____

If you could do this week over, what would you do differently?

_____
_____
_____

SLEEP THROUGH THE STORMS

Have you ever experienced the pain of seeing someone you love choose to be with another person? How did you handle it?

_____

_____

_____

If you could do that situation over, what would you do differently?

_____

_____

_____

Russ tells Jason, "love is patient, love is kind, love bears all things, endures all things, love never ends.' Feelings come and go, but love endures forever." How does this match up with the "love" our culture talks about?

_____

_____

_____

Russ tells Jason that storms in life are inevitable, no matter if you think you are a 'good' person or not. What do you need to do to prepare for the storms?

_____

_____

_____

What was your takeaway from the story about the sailor?

_____

_____

_____

Have you ever been afraid to reach out and talk with someone because you were afraid of looking weak? If you are going through that now, please talk with a trusted person in your life rather than keep it all inside.

_____

_____

_____

CAN'T CHEAT THE PERSON IN THE MIRROR

What does it mean to be intentional about using social media? Give an example of a time your compared your life to a life you saw on social media. How did this make you feel?

_____

_____

_____

What are mirror neurons? How do you think they impact your life?

_____

_____

_____

Jan tells Jason, "The hard truth is that so often, what we see in others says a lot more about us than it does about them." When you think about what you see in others, what does this mirror reveal about you?

_____

_____

_____

Jan tells Jason, _"You can cheat a lot of people in this life, but you can never cheat the person in the mirror."_ Have you ever experienced this? Where in your life are you currently cheating yourself?

_____

_____

_____

CIRCUMSTANCE AND BEING

Why do you believe so many people who played in the NBA go broke within 5 years of finishing their career?

_____

_____

_____

What's the difference between a transformation of circumstance and transformation of being? Have you ever seen an example of this?

_____

_____

_____

What was your takeaway from the three types of transformation Augie shared?

_____

_____

_____

_____

_____

_____

_____

AUTHENTIC VULNERABILITY

Do you ever feel the need or temptation to only show your highlight reel on social media?

_____

_____

_____

Russ admits to Jason, "Often times when we are feeling inadequate or not good enough, we will try and project an image of success or things 'looking good' in order to try and cover up our true feelings. A king, a queen, or any truly powerful person never needs to tell you they are powerful, they just are. When I was in my 30's I struggled with this a lot. To create that image of success, I wore designer clothes and drove a Ferrari. I had worked very hard to build a significant brand and I wanted other people to know how successful I was. But as I've already told you, inside I was a mess. Every day I desperately tried to cover up my own feelings of worthlessness." What are your thoughts about this? Have you ever experienced what Russ is sharing?

_____

_____

_____

_____

_____

_____

Russ tells Jason that truly successful people *"live with radically authentic vulnerability, because they know that the world always connects more with your grit than your shine. They might show up for the shine, but they will stay because of your grit.*" What does this mean to you?

_____

_____

_____

Think about your interactions with the other people, do you make other people feel big, or do you make other people feel small? Is that who you want to be? Are there any ways you can improve in this area?

_____

_____

_____

_____

_____

_____

_____

A ROUGH START

Have you ever had a coach, boss, or teacher who you felt like had no clue what they were doing? How did you handle it? What would you do differently if you could do it all over again?

_____

_____

_____

What are three things that you can do that are beneficial and constructive to get better *even if* you have a leader that is incompetent?

_____

_____

_____

PERSPECTIVE

Have you ever experienced a team with a "loss of heart"? What can you do to help make things better in a situation like this?

_____

_____

_____

Who in your life helps you gain perspective on what truly matters in life and what doesn't?

_____

_____

_____

How can you live with the type of reckless love and joy that Ryan does? What do you think is stopping you from doing it?

_____

_____

_____

Andy Andrews says, "perspective is the only thing that can dramatically change the results without changing any of the facts." What are three things you can do to gain perspective when you are losing it?

_____

_____

_____

Commitment Card: Week 8

Start Date: _____ End Date: _____

I want to develop this characteristic:

_____

In order to help ensure that I develop that I am going to commit to:

_____

_____

_____

I want to develop this characteristic:

_____

In order to help ensure that I develop that I am going to commit to:

_____

_____

_____

I want to develop this skill:

_____

In order to help ensure that I develop that I am going to commit to:

_____

_____

_____

I want to develop this skill:

_____

In order to help ensure that I develop that I am going to commit to:

_____

_____

_____

What was your best failure this week?

_____

_____

_____

If you could do this week over, what would you do differently?

_____

_____

_____

CONTROL THE CONTROLLABLES

Russ tells Jason, "Whether you win or lose is not controllable. You want to believe it is. Everything you've been taught and led to believe tells you that it is. But that's a lie. Jason, our society is obsessed with winning and losing, but you can't control that." Do you agree or disagree with this statement? Why?

_____

_____

_____

Russ spouts off a long list of things it takes no natural ability to do. What are three things that he mentioned that are specific to your craft? Are there things that he missed?

_____

_____

_____

Russ tells Jason, "In life you are going to come across challenging situations in the forms of people who are serving as teachers, coaches, bosses, even parents sometimes, but the truth is that you still have a choice to focus on the controllables. You still have a choice to determine the meaning you are going to give that experience. A lot of kids your age quit every time they experience a hard coach, or even a bad coach. But can you see how if you change your perspective and choose to focus on what you can control and lean into it, that it can help you develop the grit and character you are going to need for later on in life?" What are some of the experiences in your life that you would benefit from changing the negative meaning you have given them?

_____

_____

_____

NO WAY OUT

Have you ever allowed a moment of temporary pain to allow you to make a poor decision? What did it end up costing you? If it didn't end up costing you much, what *could* it have cost you?

_____

_____

_____

What are at least three things you could do that are more beneficial ways of handling the emotional pain and frustration?

_____

_____

_____

_____

_____

_____

_____

IT IS WHAT IT IS

Have you ever felt like no matter how hard you try, you are 'just a statistic'?

_____

_____

_____

How did it make you feel when you found out that Russ had come through for Jason? Why do you think he did it?

_____

_____

_____

_____

_____

_____

_____

Russ tells Jason, "You have greatness inside of you, but you have to choose between it and excuses. You can't have both. _The greatness inside of you is buried underneath all your excuses and rationalizations._" If you are honest with yourself, what are some of the legitimate excuses you lean on that are holding you back?

_____

_____

_____

_____

_____

_____

_____

Russ tells Jason, "Even though you have legitimate excuses and rationalizations, it doesn't change this truth. *Everyone comes to a point in their life and they have to decide in that moment who they are going to be. Who they are going to become. You can't allow anyone else to decide that for you.*" What does this mean to you? Who do you want to become?

_____

_____

_____

_____

_____

_____

WHOLE ON THE INSIDE

Have you ever obsessed about something to only later realize that it wasn't really about that thing at all, but rather something deeper underneath the surface?

_____

_____

_____

Have you ever felt like you are missing out on something in life? How did this chapter impact your perspective?

_____

_____

_____

Matthew Kelly says the "*go out and get what you want---and you'll be happy*' is a failed experiment. You can never get enough of what you don't need." What do you think about this?

_____

_____

_____

Have you ever gotten something or experienced something you thought was going to change everything, to realize it doesn't change much at all?

_____

_____

_____

NO SHORTCUTS

Have you ever thought you found a shortcut, Only to find it actually set you back in life? What did you learn from this?

_____

_____

_____

What was your takeaway from learning that over 75% of sales are made somewhere between the fifth and twelfth contact? How does this apply to your craft and your process?

_____

_____

_____

Russ tells Jason, "There are no shortcuts to sustained greatness. It takes what it takes." He also tells him about how long it took John Legend to get signed. In what areas of your craft do you need to develop world class patience?

_____

_____

_____

PLAYING PRESENT

Now that you are over half way through the story, what does the Stonecutter's Credo mean to you and your craft? "...*yet at the hundred and first blow it will split in two and I know that it was not that blow that did it, but all that had gone before.*"

_____

_____

_____

_____

_____

Where do you tend to spend the majority of time in your head, the past, present, or future?

_____

_____

_____

What are some of the distraction that keep you from living present? What are three things you can do to live more present?

_____

_____

_____

_____

_____

Commitment Card: Week 9

Start Date: _____ End Date: _____

I want to develop this characteristic:
_____

_____

In order to help ensure that I develop that I am going to commit to:
_____

_____

_____

I want to develop this characteristic:
_____

In order to help ensure that I develop that I am going to commit to:
_____

_____

_____

I want to develop this skill:
_____

In order to help ensure that I develop that I am going to commit to:
_____

_____

_____

I want to develop this skill:
_____

In order to help ensure that I develop that I am going to commit to:

_____

_____

_____

What was your best failure this week?

_____

_____

_____

If you could do this week over, what would you do differently?

_____

_____

_____

HUMBLE & HUNGRY

Do some research on "flow." What does flow mean to you?

_____

_____

_____

What are at least two ways you can increase the likelihood of entering into a flow state more often?

_____

_____

_____

T.D. tells Jason, "the byproduct of greatness isn't ego: it's humility. The best in the world always have a healthy, humble respect for the game and their opponent. _You want to always stay humble and hungry. There is always more to learn and always room to grow. Mastery isn't a destination, it is a continual process and never ending journey in this life._" What are your thoughts on this?

_____

_____

_____

What is the difference between cocky and confident?

_____

_____

_____

C.S. Lewis says, "humility is not thinking less of yourself, but in thinking of yourself less." Is this the way humility is taught and conditioned in our culture?

_____

_____

_____

10,000 DOORS

Have you ever felt the gratification of finishing something really hard? How did it feel?

_____

_____

_____

What do you gain by taking the hard way instead of the easy path in life?

_____

_____

_____

"BE A MAN."

If you are a male, how has the phrase "be a man" impacted your life? If you are a female, how has that phrase impacted the males in your life?

_____

_____

_____

What were your thoughts on the "be a man" box Russ did with Jason? Do you agree?

_____

_____

_____

What happens in a culture where males will do anything to stay in the "be a man" box?

_____

_____

_____

What do you think it means to truly be a man?

_____

_____

_____

_____

_____

CAPTAIN

Have you ever been tempted to quit on the process that led you to positive things happening in your life? How do you sustain the process once you start to experience those positive things?

_____

_____

_____

Have you ever seen one person turn around a culture because of their willingness to courageously go it alone until others start to join? Are there any areas on your team where you need to step up and be that person?

_____

_____

_____

Do you need a title like "captain" or "manager" to effectively lead?

_____

_____

_____

FINALLY

Have you ever had some find the courage to share something really vulnerable from their life with you? How did it make you feel towards them? Did it strengthen your bond or repulse you?

_____

_____

_____

Have you ever told someone how you felt and been rejected? Did this stop you from being vulnerable and courageous in the future?

_____

_____

_____

Gary Vee says, "we only get one at bat at life, so roll up on the hot chick and ask her out, build your business, make that thing, but don't get to the end of your life with regret. Regret is poison." What are at least three things you know in your gut you should do, not necessarily so you will get what you want, but so that you will become the type of person that lives without regret?

_____

_____

_____

Commitment Card: Week 10

Start Date: _____ End Date: _____

I want to develop this characteristic:

_____

In order to help ensure that I develop that I am going to commit to:

_____

_____

_____

I want to develop this characteristic:

_____

In order to help ensure that I develop that I am going to commit to:

_____

_____

_____

I want to develop this skill:

_____

In order to help ensure that I develop that I am going to commit to:

_____

_____

_____

I want to develop this skill:

_____

In order to help ensure that I develop that I am going to commit to:

_____

_____

_____

What was your best failure this week?

_____

_____

_____

If you could do this week over, what would you do differently?

_____

_____

_____

GOING FIRST

Have you every unexpectedly found yourself in a leadership role you didn't feel ready for? How did you handle it? If you could do it all over again, what would you do differently?

_____

_____

_____

What does it feel like to have a leader that constantly blames and rarely takes responsibility?

_____

_____

_____

What does "extreme ownership" mean to you?

_____

_____

_____

What gets in the way of you being "authentically vulnerable"? What do you think that is costing you?

_____

_____

_____

COURAGE IS CONTAGIOUS

Have you ever experienced the effect of 'going first' and sharing with a group about hard stuff? What happened after you did that? What did you learn from this experience?

_____

_____

_____

What masks do you wear every day? If you could take them off without fear of what might happen, what would you want people to know about you?

_____

_____

_____

Have you or someone you've known come from an environment like Travis where nothing is ever good enough? Why is that dangerous?

_____

_____

_____

How do you think "perfectionism" affects people's ability to work? Does it help them fulfill their potential?

_____

_____

_____

Read the following excerpt from Art and Fear, by David Bayles and Ted Orland, then discuss the implications.

"The ceramics teacher announced on opening day that he was dividing the class into two groups. All those on the left side of the studio, he said, would be graded solely on the quantity of work they produced, all those on the right solely on its quality.

His procedure was simple: on the final day of class he would bring in his bathroom scales and weigh the work of the "quantity" group: fifty pound of pots rated an "A", forty pounds a "B", and so on. Those being graded on "quality", however, needed to produce only one pot"albeit a perfect one"to get an "A".

Well, came grading time and a curious fact emerged: the works of highest quality were all produced by the group being graded for quantity. It seems that while the "quantity" group was busily churning out piles of work"and learning from their mistakes"the "quality" group had sat theorizing about perfection, and in the end had little more to show for their efforts than grandiose theories and a pile of dead clay."

_____

_____

_____

_____

_____

_____

_____

_____

CHANGING THE ECHOES

In what ways do you see bullying impact your team?

_____

_____

_____

_____

_____

_____

Kaiya tells Jason, "Real men don't need to make others feel small in order to make themselves look big." What do you think about this statement?

_____

_____

_____

_____

_____

What are two or three specific things you can do to change the echoes inside of your organization?

_____

_____

_____

_____

_____

RESISTANCE

Have you ever experienced social shame when you started making positive changes in your life?

_____

_____

_____

How do you see the "crab mentality" play out in your world?

_____

_____

_____

Kaiya tells Jason, "Even though the man you're becoming is a much stronger, more capable, more empathetic person, they'll fight that transformation every step of the way. Because every step is like a mirror for their own insecurities and shortcomings. You guys grew up on the same block. And if you can change, it means that they can too, if they only had the grit, courage, and discipline to do so. But they would rather believe that they're the victims of their circumstances, and that change is impossible, because that means they can go on living how they have been and not think about it. Change is scary, and you shouldn't be surprised when some people in your life resist it, instead of celebrate it." Have you ever seen this play out in your life or someone around you? What are some beneficial strategies for handling the social shame you will experience when you make positive changes?

_____

_____

_____

Kaiya tells Jason, "*there are no extraordinary people, just ordinary people willing to experience shame, persecution, and even death to pursue what sets their soul on fire.*" Who are some examples of people in your life who fit this description?

_____

_____

_____

_____

_____

_____

SWEEP THE SHEDS

What would it look like for you to 'Sweep The Sheds"?

_____

_____

_____

How have you seen success be a double edged sword?

_____

_____

_____

WHO DO YOU WANT TO BE?

Have you ever hurt someone you care deeply about over something that really doesn't matter? How can you help to maintain a focus on what truly matters to lower the likelihood of you doing this in the future?

_____

_____

_____

_____

_____

What were your takeaways from the story about Brandon?

_____

_____

_____

_____

Do you believe like Russ said that the process matters more than any outcome? Why?

_____

_____

_____

_____

_____

Commitment Card: Week 11

Start Date: _____   End Date: _____

I want to develop this characteristic:

_____

In order to help ensure that I develop that I am going to commit to:

_____

_____

_____

I want to develop this characteristic:

_____

In order to help ensure that I develop that I am going to commit to:

_____

_____

_____

I want to develop this skill:

_____

In order to help ensure that I develop that I am going to commit to:

_____

_____

_____

I want to develop this skill:

_____

In order to help ensure that I develop that I am going to commit to:

_____

_____

_____

What was your best failure this week?

_____

_____

_____

If you could do this week over, what would you do differently?

_____

_____

_____

THE FUTURE

Close your eyes and take a few deep breathes, then put your hand over your heart as you continue breathing deeply. Then think about if there is anyone you need to apologize to. Write out a plan of how and when you will do it.

_____

_____

_____

_____

_____

_____

Have you ever been around someone so wrapped up in their world that they couldn't even notice the pain in your world? How did that make you feel? How can you take steps to limit doing this in other people's lives?

_____

_____

_____

_____

_____

_____

GOING TO THE SHIP

What are some practical examples of what each of these things might look like in your life?

Focus → On playing for your teammates rather than your shots, feelings, or pain

Fight → For all the little inches

Finish → Empty

_____

_____

_____

_____

_____

_____

Have you ever experienced a serious setback in one of your biggest moments? How did you respond? If you could do it all over again, what would you do differently?

_____

_____

_____

_____

_____

_____

THE STONE SPLITS

After going through this training manual and book, do you feel like you can sleep through the storms? If not, what changes do you still need to make?

_____

_____

_____

_____

_____

_____

How did it make you feel not knowing whether he missed or made the final shot? Why do you think the author wrote it that way?

_____

_____

_____

_____

_____

_____

YOU AREN'T ENTITLED TO YOUR DREAMS

In what ways have you been impacted by "safe" jobs becoming extinct?

_____

_____

_____

Russ tells Jason, "You must experiment and fail over and over again as you put the wisdom into practice in your life. It's not good enough to just hear wisdom, or read it, you must perpetually go and learn how it works in the real world by attempting to use it over and over again." What do you need to start or continue experimenting with in your life?

_____

_____

_____

What do you know in your gut that you are supposed to build, pursue, or chase that other people think is foolish?

_____

_____

_____

What would it look like for you to become relentless in the pursuit of what sets your soul on fire?

_____

_____

_____

What would it look like in your life for you to choose love and courage over fear and shame?

_____

_____

_____

I would love to hear your top 7 lessons from the book, and the overall impact the book and this training manual have had on your life! ☺

You can also download the *Pound The Stone* motivational mixtape at t2bc.com

Love,

Joshua Michael Medcalf

Twitter: @joshuamedcalf
Instagram: @realjoshuamedcalf
Email: Joshua@traintobeclutch.com
Cell: 918-361-8611

BRING THE *POUND THE STONE* MESSAGE TO YOUR ORGANIZATION

Keynote | *Video Program*

Discussion Guide | *Offsite Workshop*

Visit www.poundthestone.com for more information.

If you are interested in more ideas for implementing the Pound The Stone philosophy, lessons, leadership, or mental skills with high school or middle school teams or groups, please contact lucas@traintobeclutch. com He is our resident ninja with implementing the t2bc curriculum with young kids.

MORE BOOKS BY JOSHUA MEDCALF

Chop Wood Carry Water, is the story of a young boy named John, who embarks upon a ten-year journey to live his dream of becoming a samurai warrior. Lessons on mental training, leadership, and life-skills are woven into the storyline as John progresses through his journey to fulfill his dream. This story will captivate your attention and help you understand the importance of, and how to, fall in love with the process of becoming great. A quick read at only 120 pages, its simple story with deep themes engage kids and adults alike. When people ask where to start with mental training, we encourage them to start with *Chop Wood Carry Water*, as it will lay the foundation in a super practical way. It is the book I would have given anything to have had growing up.

Chop Wood Carry Water is a viral sensation and we are confident that you too will fall in love with the process of becoming great as you go on a journey with John.

We are living through one of the greatest shifts and redistribution of power our country has ever seen. Many people have failed to see that beneath their political frustrations the shifts really have to do with the disruption caused by technology. Casey Neistat has turned down multiple offers from companies like HBO and SHOWTIME, because he generates more views on YouTube than they typically get for their shows. Last year, I turned down a six figure publishing deal, because my book Chop Wood Carry Water was a viral sensation that didn't need a traditional publisher to make a big splash in the marketplace. The tribe I had built on social media gave me the leverage and confidence to be able to say "no thank you." Every day jobs that used to be safe are becoming harder to find or disappearing all together. Then finally, when ESPN announced it was making massive layoffs and it became clear that my kids might grow up without it, I realized just how fast this shift was happening. Much like the guy with Aspergers in The Big Short, I have been seeing how many areas of our economy: education, advertising, media, and entertainment, just to name a few, are being propped up artificially and are a house of cards ready to collapse.

In November of 2016 I gave a keynote presentation at an event in Australia called, *Money In Sport.* I had landed in Sydney, Australia to find out Donald Trump was the next president of the United States. Four days later, I spoke about how the thing I learned from the election was that traditional media's influence is a dinosaur unaware that it is about to become extinct.

I wrote the book, *Hustle,* as my entrepreneurial memoir with all the lessons and failures I learned along the way. In order to thrive, and possibly even survive this new world we are living in, you must learn to think and act like an entrepreneur. In this book, I teach you how.

Many people who have read all of our books believe that, *Transformational Leadership*, is our secret gem. Originally it was released with a different title and for whatever reason it did not sell that many copies. We didn't think too much about it, and just moved on writing new books. But then like a cult classic that flops at the box office, people who were reading it came back to us blown away at what was happening in their life after reading it.

In this book we really try and help people move from transactional leadership to transformational leadership. In the insta-everything world we live in today, it is easy to lose focus on your mission and start treating people like production units instead of treating them like people. However, this actually undercuts your results, because no one likes to work for, play for, or be around people that don't treat them like people.

In our experience working with founders of billion dollar companies, professional sports teams, division one coaches, and everyone in between, there is a lot of talk about transformational leadership, but not very many people who are living it. Transformational leadership isn't sexy, soft, or easy.

Burn Your Goals is the first book we wrote that put T2BC on the map. It is a highly countercultural book that helps people understand the importance of shifting from living a goal driven, achievement driven, life, to living a mission driven life. This book is a tome, but only the first 50 pages focuses on the concept of Burn Your Goals. I get really frustrated at books that should have only been 50-75 pages, but because the publisher requires it, the book continues for another 200 pages. This book is not like that. It combines many other stories and ideas that delve into leadership, life-skills, and mental training.

"On a quit night in the C-Suite of Axis Medical Group, Brian Kelly holds a ten-pound sledgehammer, standing in front of a massive corner office. Staring back at him is his own name, etched across the door in polished block letters. He worked for twenty-five years to get it there, but tonight that has to change. And so, with every ounce of his strength... Brian starts to swing."

We're entering an era that will become to be known as the age of the network, a world of hyper-connectivity and constant flux, where disruption is the norm and autonomy, empowerment, and meaning are basic expectations of the new workforce. The challenge leaders face today is the fact that we live in a half-changed world, where everything from communication and etiquette, policies and procedures, where and when work happens, and "paying your dues" are still influenced by a long list of unwritten rules established by the world that preceded the Network: the Hierarchy. Successfully navigating the challenge of thriving in two very different worlds is the mandate of the modern day leader. This book will show you how.

⁓

Drawing on their years guiding everyone from Fortune 500 executives to major-league coaches through the new world of work, Seth Mattison and Joshua Medcalf combine timeless wisdom with timely strategy in, *The War At Work*, a fable grounded in two leaders' introspective journey from the top down world of the hierarchy to the hyper connected world of the Network.

If you are like me, when you have a question, you want an answer. When you are unsure of what direction to go, you want someone to lay out the perfect path for you. We spend massive amounts of time in books, articles, videos, courses, and education seeking these answers. No doubt, you hope to find some here. But here's the reality: No book has THE answers.

The answer you need, and will find, is not what you seek. Because it's in our search for answers that we develop the characteristic of accruing wisdom. In becoming someone who passionately accrues wisdom, we must apply wisdom. For, in the application of wisdom, we are transformed. And it's this transformation we undergo in our journey that is truly the answer.

It's not the answer we were looking for, but it's the answer that allows us to be effective in the world and transformational to and for those around us. When you read this book, you will not underline the answers. You will find wisdom and principles to be applied. Apply the wisdom, and become the answer.

WANT TO GO DEEPER?

Mentorship Program- Our mentorship program isn't a good fit for everyone, but we are always willing to see if it is a good fit for you. It is a serious investment of time and resources. Email Joshua@traintobeclutch.com for more information.

T2BC Reading Challenge- People are consistently telling us how going through our reading challenge has radically improved their business, family, and personal life. It is available to download under the *free stuff* tab at t2bc.com

The Experience- *Transformational Leadership Retreats.* We bring together people from all over the country to engage in a day of interactive learning. We also create space for fun activities like golf, surfing, or snowboarding with the t2bc team.

T2BC 101 Online Video Course- With over 20 short video sessions, you can use this course individually or to teach your team the T2BC curriculum. It is a great next step tool. Available at **t2bc.com/training**

Join the T2BC community- This is the best way for us to provide consistent value to your life and for us to develop a long term relationship. You will get articles, mp3's, videos, and other tools as they come out. It's also free. Join at t2bc.com

Books- Email info@traintobeclutch.com for bulk discount quotes.

YouTube- Our channel is *train2bclutch*

CPSIA information can be obtained
at www.ICGtesting.com
Printed in the USA
BVHW031813051119
562988BV00001B/110/P